MOSQUE

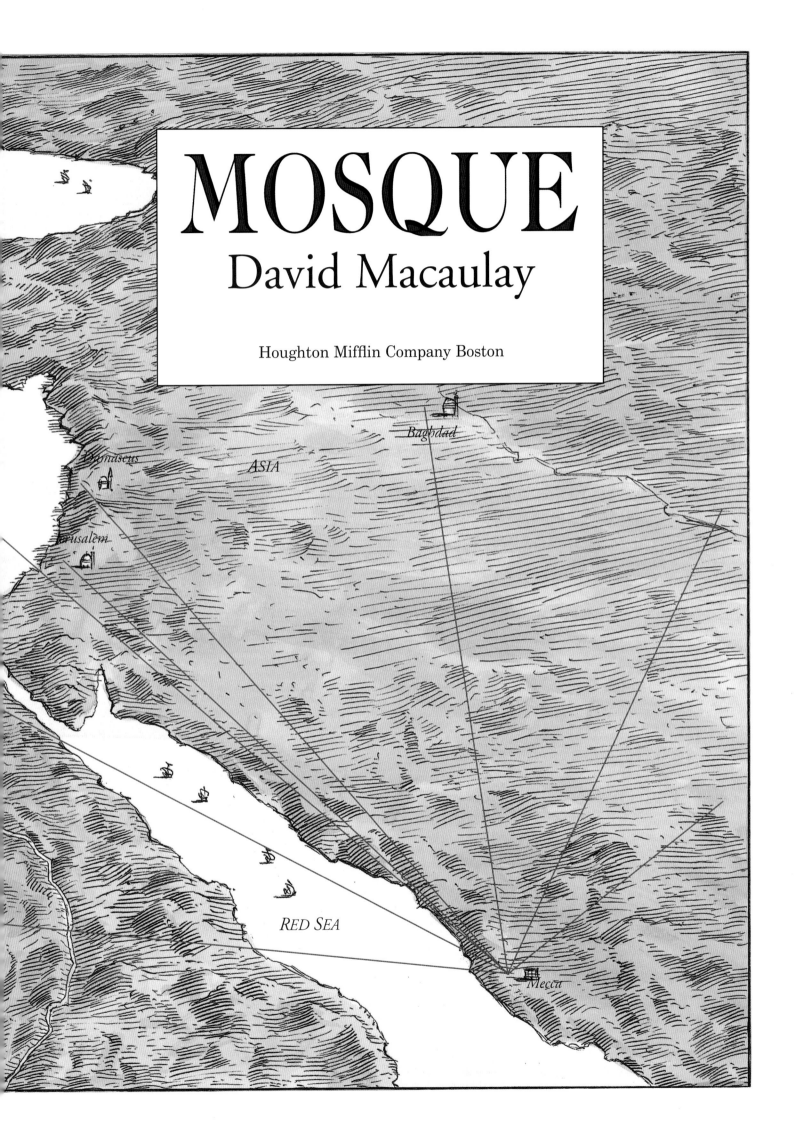

MOSQUE
David Macaulay

Houghton Mifflin Company Boston

For my children and their children's children

PREFACE

The building complex in this story is fictional, as are its patron and architect. The individual structures, however, are modeled directly on existing examples built between 1540 and 1580 in and around Istanbul, Turkey, by Sinan, the most famous architect of the Ottoman Empire.

In piecing together the various construction details I was introduced to a number of books on a subject I quickly realized I knew very little about. I was convinced, however, that the time had come to find out where these extraordinary buildings came from, who built them, why, and of course how. Those looking for more information on Sinan, mosques, or Ottoman architecture should treat themselves to books either written or edited by Dogan Kuban, Aptulla Kuran, Godfrey Goodwin, Hans G. Egli, the family Uluengin, Martin Frishman and Hasan-Uddin Khan, John Freely, Marcus Hattstein and Peter Delius, Rowland J. Mainstone, and Reha Gunay.

For their personal contributions to this journey, I would particularly like to thank the filmmaker Suha Arin, Professors Suphi Saatchi, architect M.Sc., Gulsun Tanyeli, and Ilknur Kolay at the Istanbul Technical University, architects Bulent and Mehmet Bengu Uluengin, Professor Hasan-Uddin Khan, and my guide and connection to almost all those listed above, fixer and friend Akif Ergulec. Closer to home, my thanks to our neighbor Kathryn Swanson who was always willing to put down her trowel or hat boxes for an on-demand objective comment. And last but not least, here in the trenches with me, thanks to my long suffering wife, Ruthie, who managed to maintain her critical eye long after mine was of dubious reliability. Without her steady support this book would still be on the drawing board.

It seems to me that the best examples of religious architecture are among humankind's proudest accomplishments. When working in the service of some higher entity, we humans seem capable of surpassing our reach and perhaps even our expectations. Motivated by faith, but guided ultimately by common sense, these builders created constructions that reveal a level of ingenuity, ambition, and craftsmanship rarely found in secular architecture. The greatest achievement of these buildings, however, as well as the ultimate indication of their success, lies in their ability to impress and move even those whose personal beliefs they do not necessarily serve.

Printed in China
SCP 20 19 18 17 16 15 14 13 12 11
4500805839

Library of Congress Cataloging-in-Publication Data
Macaulay, David.
  Mosque / David Macaulay.
    p. cm.
  RNF ISBN 0-618-24034-9   PA ISBN 0-547-01547-X
  1. Mosques—Design and construction. I. Title.
  NA4670.M33 2003
  726'.2—dc21   2003000177

RNF ISBN-13 978-0-618-24034-9 PA ISBN-13 978-0-547-01547-7

Istanbul

Sea of Marmara

Dardanelles

EUROPE

ASIA

INTRODUCTION

By the middle of the sixteenth century, the Ottomans had built the largest Muslim empire in the world. With superior forces on land and sea, a series of sultans had extended its borders from Algiers in the west to Baghdad in the east, from the outskirts of Vienna in the north to beyond Mecca in the south. With the establishment of military dominance came the inevitable building of trade and cultural links, and with these spread the message of Islam and its five pillars—faith, prayer, charity, fasting, and pilgrimage.

One indication of the empire's unrivaled power was the phenomenal wealth that found its way into the sultans' treasury as well as into the pockets of Istanbul's most influential citizens. For these individuals, however, adherence to the principle of charity was further encouraged by laws that prevented the bequeathing of one's entire fortune to one's children. It became a well-established practice, therefore, for the richest members of society to endow charitable foundations to channel their personal wealth into a variety of religious, educational, social, and civic activities. In addition to a new mosque, these foundations would require a number of specific buildings all grouped into an architectural complex called a kulliye.

All of the great Ottoman buildings of the second half of the sixteenth century either were mosques or belonged to their adjacent kulliyes. Remarkably, most of these buildings were the work of one man, an engineer and architect named Sinan. As chief court architect for almost fifty years, Sinan, along with his assistants, designed and oversaw the construction of buildings, bridges, and aqueducts all across the empire. By the time of his death at the age of one hundred, he had personally served as architect for some three hundred structures in Istanbul alone.

By Sinan's time, the basic form of the Ottoman mosque was well established. It consisted of an open prayer hall—ideally a perfect cube covered by an equally perfect hemisphere-shaped dome, a covered portico, an arcaded courtyard similar in area to the prayer hall itself, a fountain, and a slender minaret (usually more than one if the mosque was built by royalty). Over time the domed cube became the standard form for all the buildings of a kulliye, regardless of their function.

While the high domes and minarets of the various mosques of Istanbul served as beacons for those wishing to pray or simply to find temporary refuge from the chaos of city life, the countless rows of smaller domes belonging to the kulliyes must have provided a reassuring sense of order in the midst of an often disorienting maze of crooked streets and disappearing alleys.

Admiral Suha Mehmet Pasa had done well by war. For more than thirty years his successful naval campaigns had made him a highly respected member of the Ottoman aristocracy, a favorite of two sultans, and a very rich man. For most of his life his eyes were firmly fixed on the borders of the empire he worked so valiantly to protect. But as another decade slipped away, he found himself confronting less familiar boundaries—those of his own mortality. As a devout Muslim, the admiral understood that all the blessings and riches that had been showered upon him were not due to his own efforts as much as to the will of God. As he plucked fruit from the trees of his beloved garden and listened to the laughter and shouts of his youngest children, he decided that the time had come to demonstrate both his faith and his gratitude in the way that had become traditional for a man of his standing. His last campaign would be undertaken on dry land and its goal would be the creation of a charitable foundation.

So it was that one October day in the year 1595, a senior member of Sultan Mehmet III's Corps of Court Architects named Akif Agha was summoned to the admiral's home. The two men met in the garden and over glasses of sweet tea talked about old battles—Agha too had been a soldier in his younger days—favorite trees, and eventually architecture. When Agha left that afternoon, he carried with him a list of the buildings that would house the activities of the admiral's proposed foundation. In addition to a mosque, with its nearby turbe or tomb, the complex would include a medrese, a college for religious education; an imaret, a soup kitchen for the preparation and serving of food; a hamam for public bathing; and a cesme, a public fountain providing fresh drinking water.

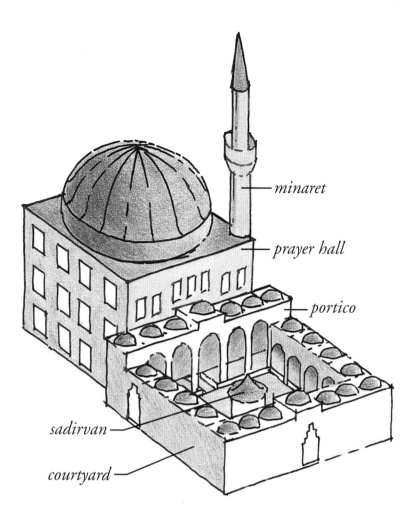

minaret

prayer hall

portico

sadirvan

courtyard

The spiritual centerpiece of the entire complex was the mosque, and the heart of the mosque was its prayer hall. It was with the design of this space in which the faithful would gather that Akif Agha began. There were a number of absolute requirements, the most important of which was that the front wall, or kibla wall, of this room must face Mecca. When praying, the congregation would assemble in rows parallel to and facing the kibla wall and in turn the holy city and its most important shrine, the Kaaba. At floor level in the center of the kibla wall was the mihrab—a niche symbolizing the entrance to paradise. It was from in front of the mihrab that the imam would lead the congregation in prayer. The kibla itself is an imaginary line that points toward and radiates from Mecca. The kibla wall was placed perpendicular to the kibla, and the mihrab stood right on top of it.

Directly opposite the mihrab was the portal—the main entrance to the prayer hall. Protecting the portal outside and providing covered space for latecomers to Friday services was a high portico, and beyond it an arcaded courtyard. In the center of the courtyard stood the sadirvan—the fountain at which the faithful would wash their hands and feet before entering the prayer hall. Like the mihrab, the main portal and the sadirvan also stood on the kibla.

The last and, next to the dome, the most recognizable element of the mosque was the tall minaret, from which the faithful would be called to prayer five times a day. It would rise from behind the portico at the northwest corner of the prayer hall.

For Akif Agha and his fellow architects and builders, there was no separation between architecture and engineering. He often reminded his young apprentices that when designing a mosque it was necessary to think from the ground up and from the top down at the same time. There were two basic problems, both of which involved the use of the dome. The first was one of geometry. How does one support a circular roof over a square room without filling the space with walls or columns? The solution that had evolved over the years was a system of piers and arches. The piers were placed either in the corners or around the perimeter of the square, and the arches tied them together. Not only did this arrangement create a suitable base for the dome above, but the space below the arches remained open and unobstructed.

The second problem was one of structure. Because of the dome's hemispherical shape, there are hidden forces within it trying to push the sides outward. While piers and arches could easily be designed to support the great weight of a masonry dome, they could not, on their own, counteract its self-destructive tendencies.

Architects reduced some of these forces by strengthening the sides of the dome, where it was most vulnerable. Then, to channel the remaining forces safely down through the piers and walls to the foundations below, they added extra weight to the tops of the piers and buttressed the arches with a symmetrical arrangement of semidomes.

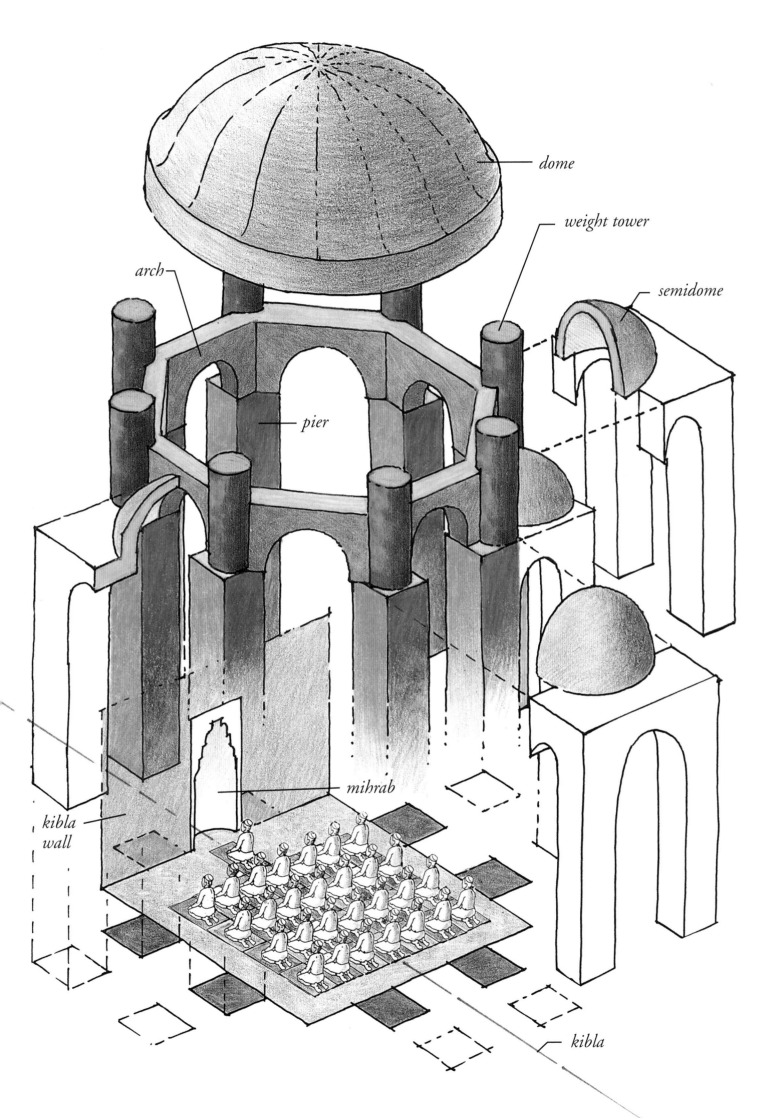

dome

weight tower

semidome

arch

pier

mihrab

kibla
wall

kibla

11

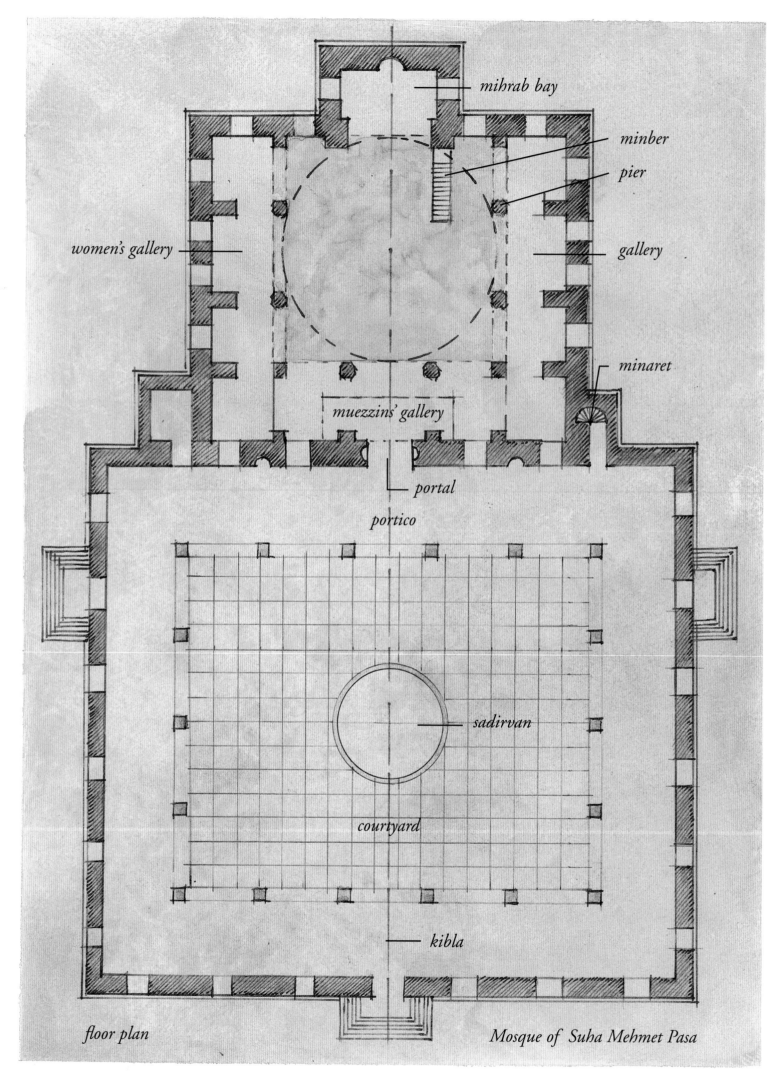

mihrab bay

minber

pier

women's gallery

gallery

minaret

muezzins' gallery

portal

portico

sadirvan

courtyard

kibla

floor plan

Mosque of Suha Mehmet Pasa

Much of the design of the admiral's mosque was based on tradition, and all of it was heavily influenced by the work of the late Sinan—once Agha's teacher as well as the former head of the Corps of Court Architects. No matter what shape the perimeter of the prayer hall ultimately took, the space at its center would remain an open square defined by the eight piers supporting the dome. To draw more attention to the mihrab, Agha set it into its own bay, which he pushed out from the central space. Then, to give as many worshipers as possible access to the kibla wall, he extended it beyond both sides of the central square. He provided raised galleries along both sidewalls—one of them for women—and a third at the rear of the prayer hall for the muezzins who would chant the words of the Koran. This mosque was to be large enough to accommodate Friday services, certainly the most important religious gathering of the week and probably the most important secular one too. The sermons at these services would be delivered from the second to last step of a high pulpit called a minber. The traditional placement of the minber was to one side of the mihrab or, in this case, the mihrab bay.

The design Agha finally presented to the admiral in January of 1596 called for a prayer hall seventy feet wide and fifty-six feet deep. The dome would be forty-two feet in diameter and its crest would stand sixty-three feet above the floor. The open courtyard space within the colonnade was roughly equal to the area of the prayer hall, and the minaret would rise to a height of one hundred ten feet. With their patron's enthusiastic approval and encouragement, Agha and his staff immediately began the detailed planning.

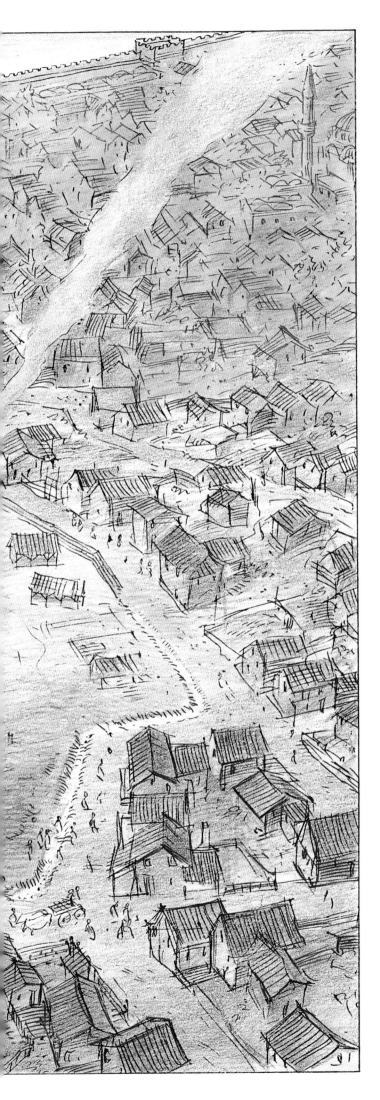

By early spring, negotiations had been concluded for a site that fulfilled all of the admiral's wishes. In addition to being obtained for a good price, it was blessed with an excellent view of the harbor and benefited from the steady breezes on which his ships had so often set sail. Not everyone shared His Excellency's nostalgia for breezes, however. All too often, these very same winds would fan small fires into raging infernos such as the one that less than ten years earlier had reduced this entire neighborhood to rubble and left its population in despair.

To oversee the day-in, day-out activities at the site, Agha hired a man named Huseyin Bey to serve as the superintendent of building. Bey soon had gangs of unskilled laborers clearing the site and digging foundation trenches for the wall that would enclose both the mosque and the medrese in a single precinct. He also set aside a space near one of the entrances to this precinct for toilets and assigned temporary areas to each of the building trades for their work sheds and supplies.

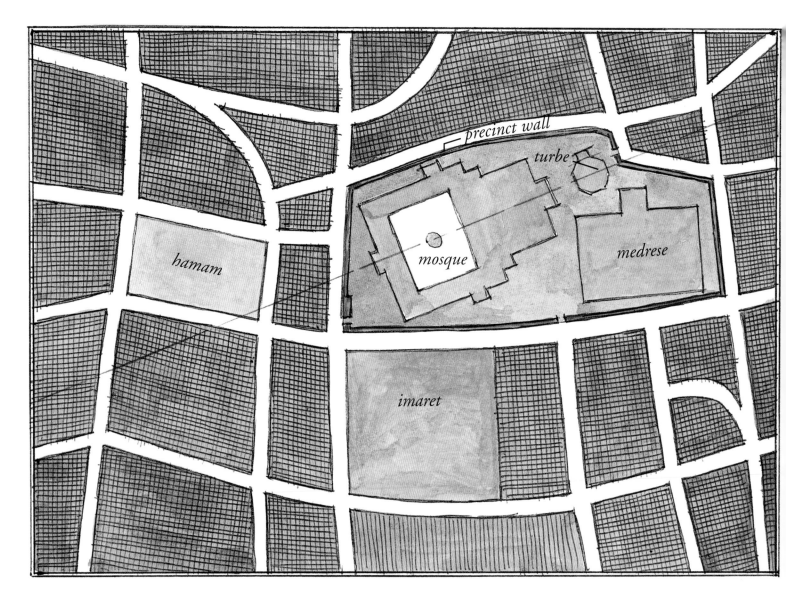

Kulliye of Suha Mehmet Pasa

Since relatively few large building projects were under way at the time, Agha had little trouble finding the necessary workers. At least half of them would be skilled craftsmen and artists, and half of this group, particularly the bricklayers and blacksmiths, would most likely be Christians. Most of the stonemasons, carpenters, roofers, and window makers would be Muslims. Hundreds of additional skilled and unskilled laborers, boatmen, wagon drivers, night watchmen, storekeepers, and porters, would also be hired. More than a thousand workers would be employed on and around the site at any given time and, to take advantage of the long summer days, that number would most certainly increase.

Early on the morning of June 5, 1596, surveyors established the placement of the kibla wall and marked it on the site with wooden stakes. They then carefully transferred Agha's plan from the paper on which it was drawn to the ground itself. Less than a week later, excavation of the deep trenches for the foundations of the prayer hall was begun. Although the admiral would occasionally express frustration with the length of time being spent on foundations that no one would ever see, Agha assured him that in a city such as Istanbul, with its long history of earthquakes, the quality of these buried walls was every bit as important as that of the walls they would support aboveground. If the admiral couldn't refute the logic of Agha's preparations, he could at least speed them up. He assigned several hundred galley slaves from a nearby garrison to help dig the trenches. Once a reliable surface had been reached, a thick level base of rubble and cement was then created, upon which the foundation walls would be built.

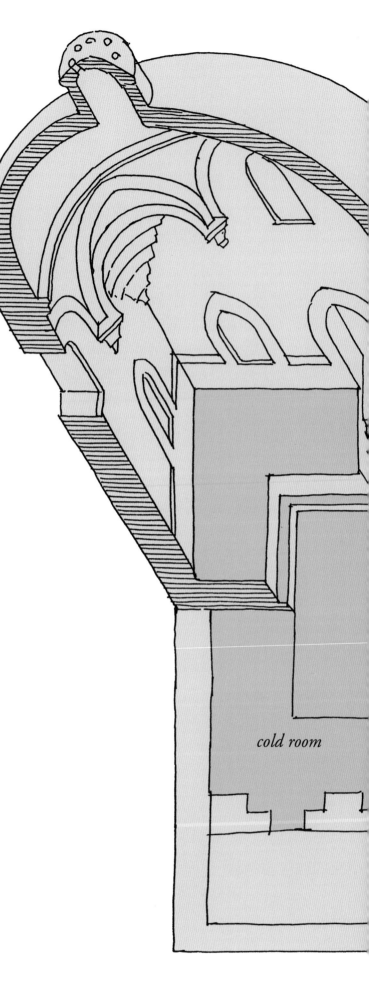

cold room

Two blocks away from the main site, near an existing well, another group of workers was digging the foundations for the hamam. The admiral had decided that the baths should be completed as soon as possible for the use of his workers. The bathhouse Agha designed followed the sequence first established in ancient times in which bathers moved from cold room to warm room to hot room. In the cold room, they would undress and relax, perhaps sipping coffee or mineral water before bathing. A fountain in the center of the room would fill the air with its soothing sound. The actual cleansing process began in the warm room and continued in the hot room, where bathers could either wash at one of the basins or simply sweat while reclining on a large heated marble platform. Those wishing to submit their bodies to the most concentrated heat would sit in one of the enclosed areas at each corner of the hot room.

The floor beneath the warm room and the hot room was to be supported above a shallow open space called a hypocaust. Hot gases from the adjacent furnace would pass through this space on the way to flues buried in the walls. An array of small chimneys on the roof could be opened or closed to regulate the flow of these gases, thereby raising or lowering the temperature of the rooms below. Hot water and steam from the boiler above the furnace was to be piped into the hot room.

heating flu

hot room

warm room

toilets

to hypocaust
furnace and boiler room

Hamam of Suha Mehmet Pasa

During the months it would take to complete both sets of foundations, Agha and his assistants spent much of their time estimating the quantities of the various building materials required, locating adequate sources, and establishing firm and acceptable prices. Only by careful planning early on could they hope to stay within the high but not infinite budget the admiral had set aside or avoid running out of a particular material at any point in process.

The most important building material was high-quality stone, much of which would come from a large quarry near the western city of Edirne. Gangs of quarrymen first pried great slabs off the cliff face and then divided them into smaller pieces. Stonecutters next chiseled these irregular lumps into rough rectangular blocks that were then loaded on carts for the 140-mile-long journey to Istanbul. Once they reached the site, these blocks would be cut to their final dimensions and dressed by master masons and their apprentices.

1.

2.

3.

4.

Another important building material was brick, much of which came from the nearby brickyard at Haskoy. There groups of men carefully mixed precise quantities of washed sand and clay, which was then carted over to one of the sheds, where skilled craftsmen molded it into bricks of various shapes and sizes. Every available piece of ground was covered by rows of wet bricks drying in the sun. After three days, these same bricks would be baked in one of the large kilns for three more days. Those to be used in the construction of walls were larger and somewhat heavier than those being produced for the domes.

By November, the streets between the site and the harbor were often impassable as one cartload of material after another slowly wound its way up the hill. In addition to roughly shaped foundation blocks, which continued to arrive from the quarries of Kadikoy, there were shipments of fine stone from Edirne, long, straight tree trunks from the forests around the Black Sea, and lime from local kilns for making mortar and cement.

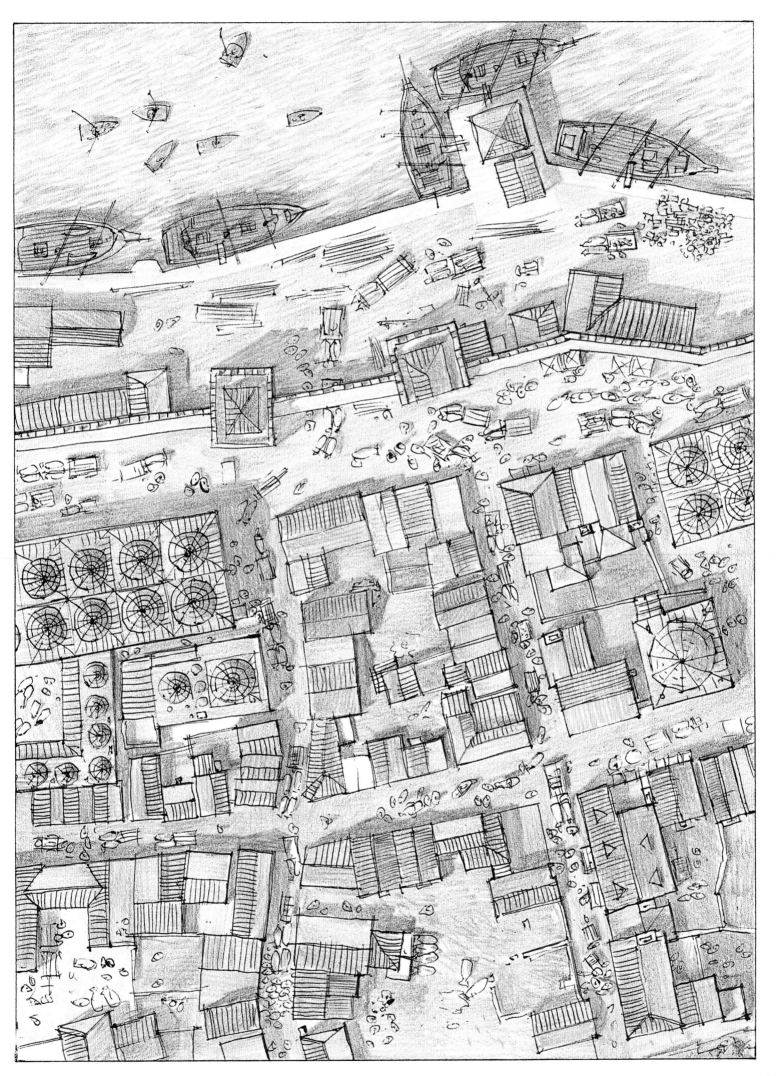

In December, traffic throughout the city was considerably hampered by layers of snow and ice. Construction of the foundations came to a complete standstill as below-freezing temperatures made it impossible to mix reliable concrete or mortar. Throughout the winter months work continued in the sheds and workshops as masons prepared thousands of square-cut stone blocks for the walls as well as marble capitals and bases for the tops and bottoms of various columns.

Jewish merchants, whose shops and offices were located along the narrow streets near the harbor, maintained a steady supply of ore from the provinces beyond Edirne. Blacksmiths working all around the city turned this ore into the thousands of connectors that would be needed to strengthen the masonry walls.

In a factory behind one such forge, workers assembled pieces of cut wrought iron into the grilles that would secure the window openings around the lower levels of the prayer hall. Sturdy rods were fastened together using specially made connectors called knots.

It wasn't until early March that work resumed on the foundations. But by that time, Bey had things so well organized that no sooner did a shipment of stone arrive on the site than it was quickly swallowed up by the waiting trenches.

Shaping a knot

By June 24 the foundations were finished. To the admiral's great delight, the future locations of each wall, pier, and column were now plainly visible. He was on hand early one morning for the ceremonial orienting of the mihrab on the foundations of the kibla wall. A ram was sacrificed and its blood was placed at each corner of the prayer hall. To express his gratitude, Suha Mehmet Pasa personally distributed presents to some of the foremen.

1.

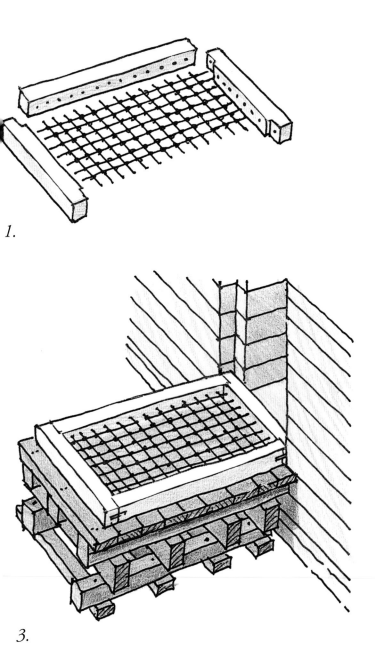

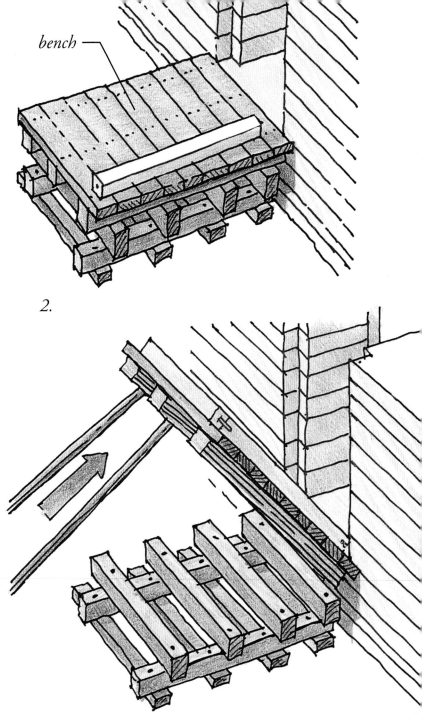

bench

2.

3.

4.

5.

Over the summer, the walls of the prayer hall rose in one continuous ring, climbing steadily toward the base of the great dome. They were faced inside and out with carefully cut stone, which the masons tied together with iron clamps and bars. To strengthen the walls further, vertical rods were inserted to bind each layer of stone to the one above it. The cavity between the inner and outer faces was filled with rubble and cement.

When the walls reached the tops of the window openings, the iron grilles were fixed in place. At the base of each opening, carpenters first erected a sturdy wooden bench upon which a grille and its surrounding stone frame were fitted together. The entire bench was then tipped upward, guiding the completed assembly into place.

centering

Using a temporary wooden frame called a centering, masons next built an arch over every window and door opening to deflect the weight safely down to the sides. As the walls rose higher and higher, scaffolding was erected along both sides to support work platforms.

By autumn, the seven bays of the portico were beginning to take shape. Since the primary purpose of the portico was to give latecomers to Friday services an appropriate place to pray, Agha had called for two niches to be built into the walls, one on each side of the portal. These would repeat the form and orientation of the mihrab. At one end of the portico, a small door opened onto a stairway leading to the women's gallery. A similar door at the opposite end led to the spiral staircase of the minaret. With its own built-in stairway, most of the minaret could be constructed without scaffolding in spite of its great height.

Four ancient marble columns, unearthed by workers digging the foundations of the hamam, were trimmed and set onto their newly carved bases. Each would support three arches. The columns at each end of the portico had to be built up in pieces since they also had to support the lower arches of the arcade that would surround the courtyard.

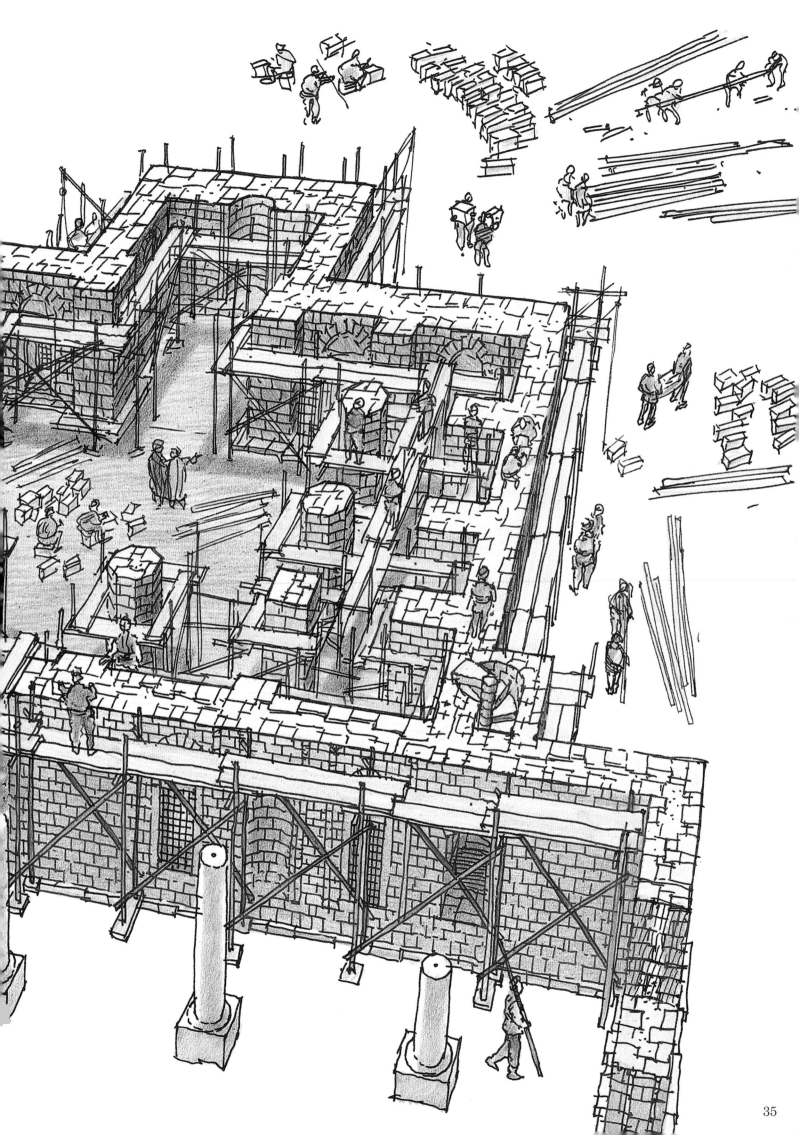

A carved marble capital was secured to the top of each column by a short iron rod. The connection between each column and capital was cushioned by a lead sheet and surrounded by a bronze ring. Once the capitals had been fastened to one another and to the walls with heavy iron tie rods, wooden centerings were hoisted into position, and the connecting arches were then built over them.

Each bay of the portico would support a dome, the centermost being raised slightly over the portal. Since each dome had to rest on a continuous circular base, triangular supports called pendentives were built out from each corner of all seven bays. The precise curvature of these pendentives was determined by using a straight wooden pole that could pivot freely from the top of a post at the center of each bay. A nail hammered into the pole at a predetermined distance from the pivot drew an imaginary arc up to which the bricks were laid. As the angle of the pole grew steeper, each successive course of bricks had to be extended a little farther into the space to meet the arc. The base of the dome was formed when the four pendentives in each bay reached the tops of the arches.

The pole was also used to establish and maintain the curvature of each dome. Unlike the bricks of the pendentives, which were laid flat, those of the domes were set at an angle. The slant of the pole helped to establish the correct slope of each brick.

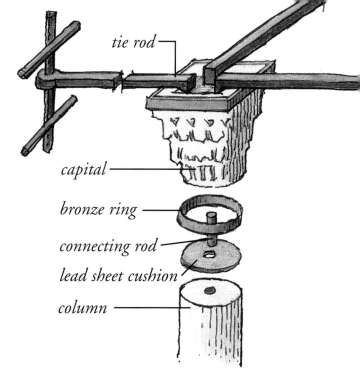

tie rod

capital

bronze ring

connecting rod

lead sheet cushion

column

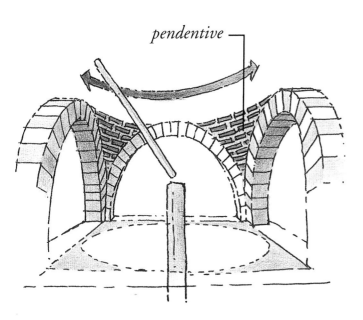

pendentive

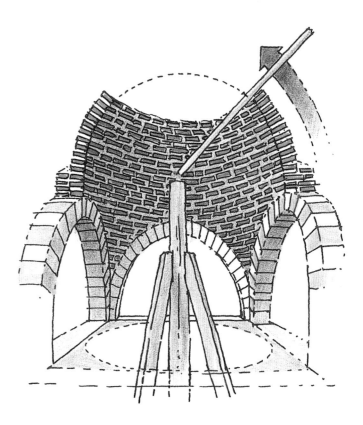

Lead sheets that would eventually cover each dome were made in a number of different workshops around the city. The master sheet maker first sprinkled a little sand over the surface of his specially built masonry bench while an assistant stirred the molten lead. When all was ready, the assistant ladled a predetermined amount into a tray at one end of the bench. The tray was then upended, spilling out its silvery contents. With a few precise movements of his board, the master carefully spread the lead to achieve a uniform thickness before it solidified. The finished sheet was still hot as it was peeled from the bench.

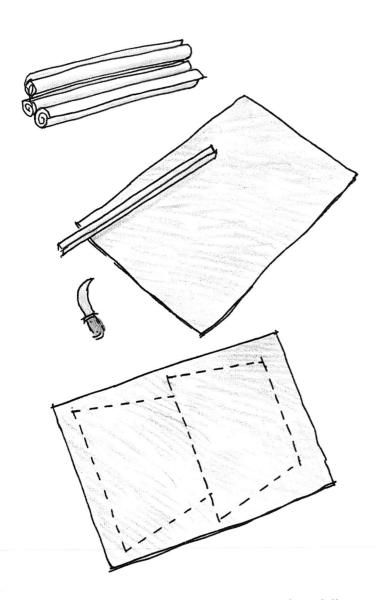

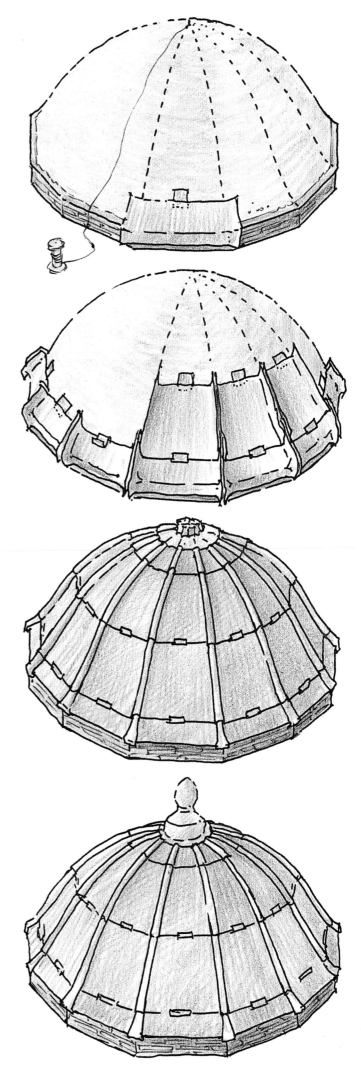

Each dome was first covered with a layer of specially prepared mud. Once hardened, this coating not only helped protect the bricks but also provided an ideal base for the lead sheets. Using a string attached to the top of the dome, the roofers scratched lines on the mud to determine the exact shape of each sheet. Beginning around the base of the dome, each sheet was nailed into place and their sides bent upward. This process was repeated until the entire dome was covered. Once all the sheets were in place, each vertical row of adjacent edges was rolled into a single seam. The cluster of seams that came together at the crest of the dome was made watertight and held in place first with a round lead collar and then with a heavy stone cap.

By December 25, the tops of most of the piers and walls stood temporarily tied together by a network of wooden centerings over which the supporting arches for the semidomes would soon be assembled.

While the prayer hall grew steadily within its man-made forest of scaffolding, the slender minaret, still completely unencumbered by such trappings, was beginning to pull away. Its builders—a group of highly skilled

40

workers who specialized in such construction and traveled together from one site to another—took great care in fitting and clamping one stone to the next. The spiral staircase itself was constructed of flat, wedge-shaped steps piled one on top of the other. The narrow end of each wedge was cut into a cylindrical shape. As the staircase rose, these stacked cylinders created a continuous central core. The wide end of each step was set into the wall, further strengthening the tower.

The first months of 1598 were unusually mild, allowing work to proceed without interruption. By March, the simpler, mostly solid walls of the hamam were almost ready to receive their domes. Agha had designed a high arch into each corner of the cold room. This increased the number of pendentives that would be required, but more importantly it reduced their size and weight. Each arch was buttressed by a small semidome.

The large domes of the cold and hot rooms were built using complete hemispherical wooden forms over which the bricks could be laid quickly and easily. The smaller domes and semidomes were built using the pole method.

By May, the bases for the semidomes of the prayer hall were complete. For additional stability, each was reinforced with a heavy iron tie rod. Various cranes and hoists were used to raise centerings and building materials to the tops of the walls in preparation for the building of the eight large arches that would eventually support the high dome. Since the minaret provided the best view of all that was going on, Akif Agha and Huseyin Bey often passed each other on the stairway. Occasionally His Excellency himself would make the long climb.

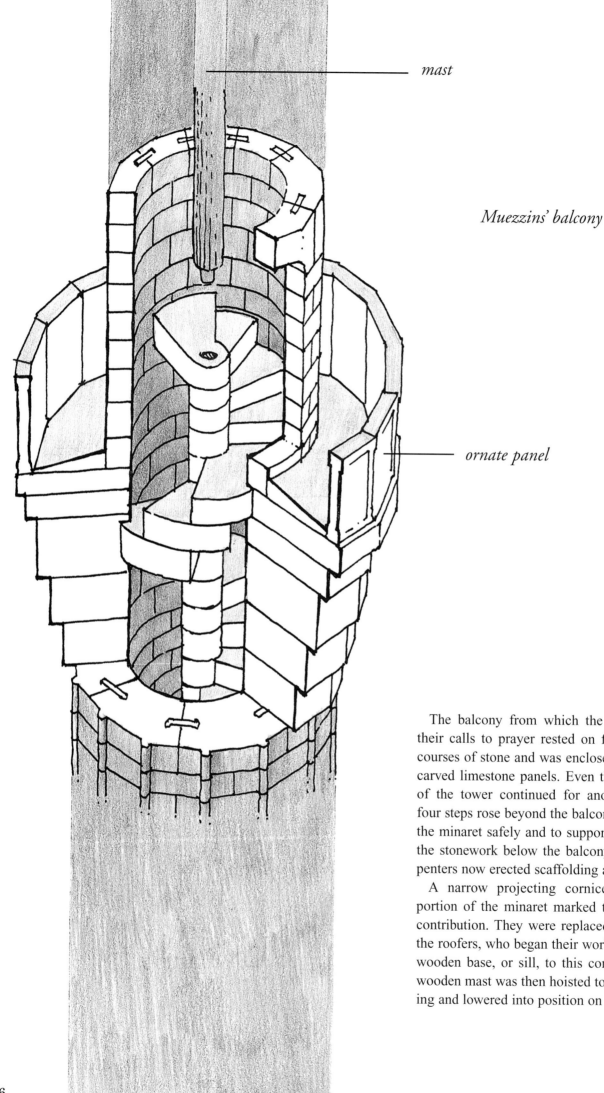

mast

Muezzins' balcony

ornate panel

The balcony from which the muezzins would issue their calls to prayer rested on five gradually widening courses of stone and was enclosed by a wall of ornately carved limestone panels. Even though the exterior wall of the tower continued for another twenty feet, only four steps rose beyond the balcony. In order to complete the minaret safely and to support platforms from which the stonework below the balcony could be carved, carpenters now erected scaffolding around the entire tower.

A narrow projecting cornice crowning the upper portion of the minaret marked the end of the masons' contribution. They were replaced on the scaffolding by the roofers, who began their work by fastening a narrow wooden base, or sill, to this cornice. A forty-foot-long wooden mast was then hoisted to the top of the scaffolding and lowered into position on the central core.

mast

cornice

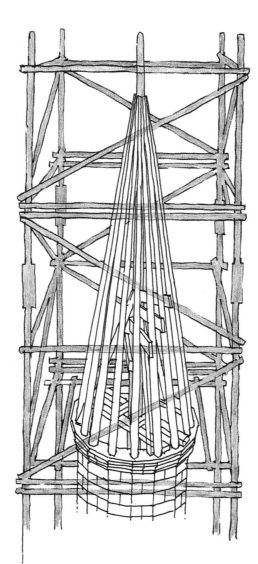

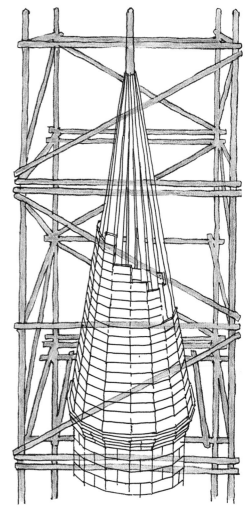

alem

The ring of long poles that would give the roof its distinct shape was installed next, followed by a layer of cladding boards and sheets of insulating felt—since mud would never have worked at such an angle. Once sheathed in lead, the graceful silver-gray cone was almost finished.

It was a clear June day when the admiral, accompanied by an officer from Queen Elizabeth's visiting fleet, stood on the muezzin's balcony. They had come to watch the pieces of the copper alem—a specially constructed finial—being stacked over the exposed tip of the mast. Before beginning their descent, the old Ottoman sailor challenged his British colleague to join him out on the scaffolding for a closer look at the intricate stalactite carving beneath the balcony.

With construction of the prayer hall well in hand, Bey was able to assign more workers to the courtyard. This enclosed, arcaded space had three entrances, one near each end of the portico and a third—slightly larger—on the kibla. The marble columns that would support the colonnade had all been shipped from Marmara Island, which was located in the sea south of the city. As the surrounding stone walls grew, window openings were built into each bay to provide pleasant views of the trees and flowers that would eventually occupy the space between the courtyard and the precinct wall. The foundations for the sadirvan and the cistern within it were dug and a pipe was laid from the nearest water tower. A second water pipe extended to the toilets at the northwest corner of the precinct. A covered channel would carry the waste and overflow out into the street drains.

By the end of September 1598, the main arches and their pendentives were finished. Small false domes were still being completed above the weight towers that now stood like sentries at each corner of the great octagon.

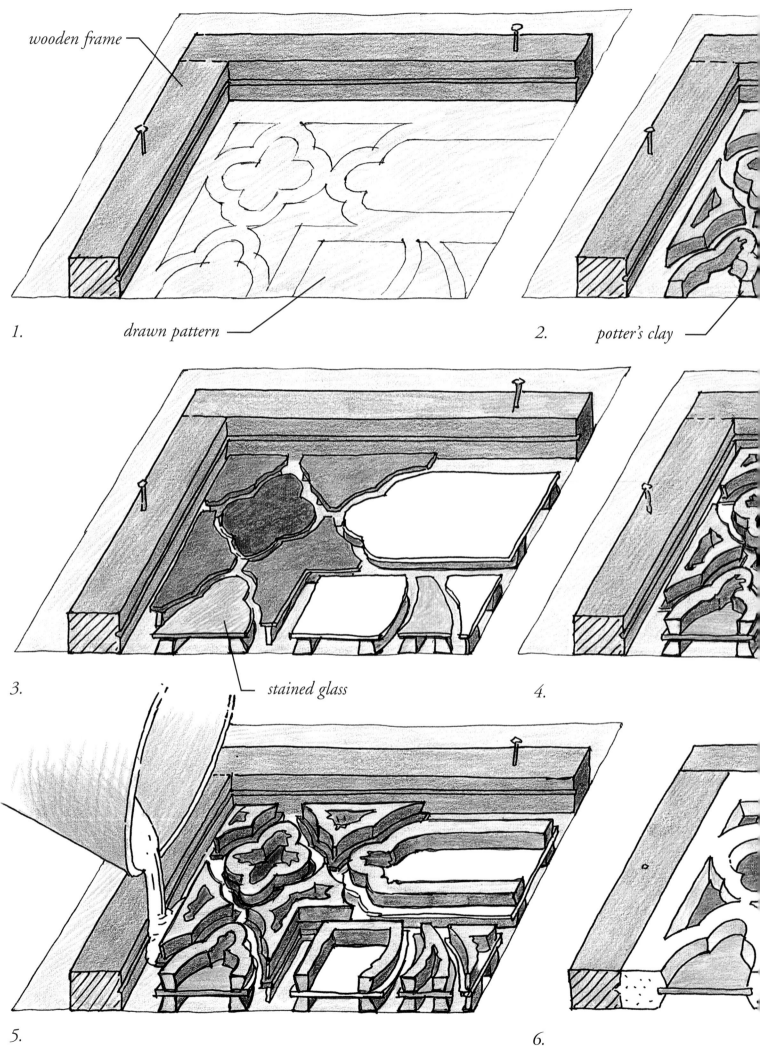

1.   *wooden frame*   *drawn pattern*

2.   *potter's clay*

3.   *stained glass*

4.

5.

6.

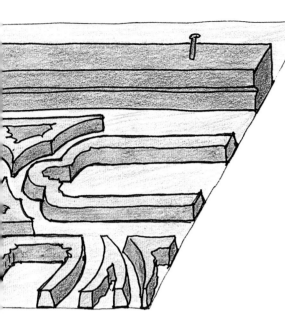

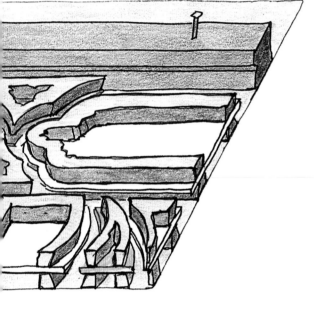

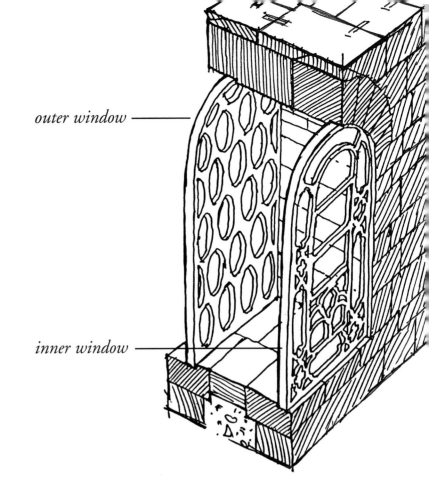

outer window ——

inner window ——

plaster —

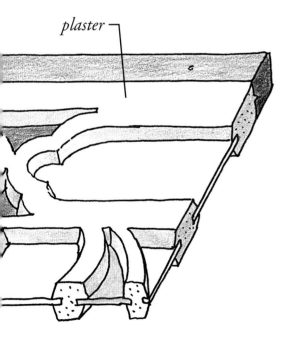

Since all the openings above the first and second level of the prayer hall were for light alone, and not ventilation, they were fitted with pairs of fixed windows. The outer windows contained only clear glass. Those on the inside were made of richly colored (and considerably more expensive) Venetian glass.

The pattern for each window was first drawn on paper and then laid out on the window maker's bench. A wooden frame that would become part of the finished window was then lightly nailed around the pattern. Thin strips of potters' clay were placed inside the frame precisely following the drawn lines. Carefully cut pieces of glass were then set on top of the clay, after which a second layer of clay strips was added. Finally, a thin mixture of plaster of Paris was poured into the cavities between the clay strips to create the tracery that holds the glass in place. Once the plaster had set to the master's satisfaction, the frame was lifted off the bench and the clay carefully scraped out. The outer windows were made the same way, but the pieces of clear glass were either round or half round, and a much more durable, cementlike mixture was used.

The window openings around the lower levels provided both light and ventilation. No glass was used in these openings, only wooden shutters hinged behind the iron grilles.

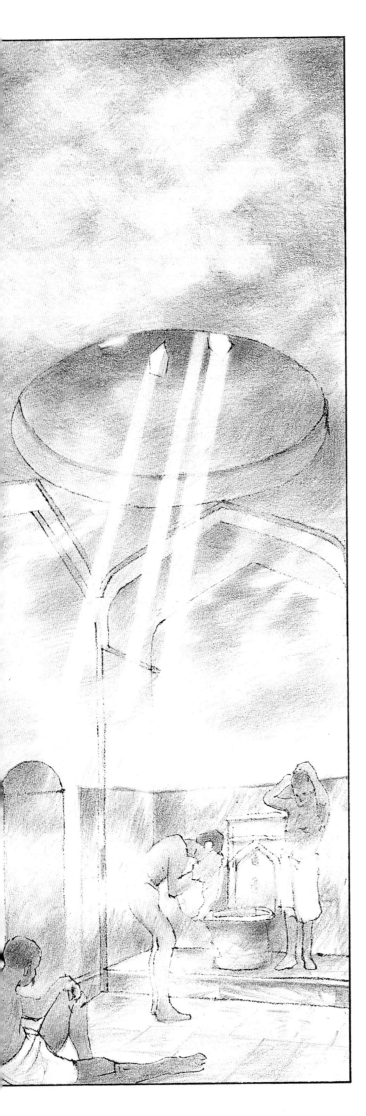

By the middle of October, the hamam was ready for its first patrons. Natural light entered the cold room through a combination of stained-glass windows set into the walls and several smaller windows contained in the cupola on top of the dome. In order to contain the heat in the hot room, no windows had been inserted into the walls. The only natural light entering this space came through small clear glass bubbles set into the dome. With the furnace fired up and the appropriate temperature reached, the admiral led his entourage into the hamam for its inaugural bath. After pronouncing the experience most satisfactory, he once again ordered that presents be distributed to the builders. Until the rest of the admiral's kulliye was finished, the baths were to serve only men. Eventually, however, an alternating schedule would be established so that both men and women could avail themselves of the waters.

Eight months later, in spite of the normal winter inter-
ruptions, presents were once again being distributed by a
grateful patron—this time to celebrate the completion of
the semidomes. From the masonry ring upon which the
high dome itself would soon rise, Agha directed the
admiral's attention to the foundation work already under
way for both the adjacent medrese and the imaret just
across the road.

The basic layout of both the medrese and the imaret were quite similar—rows of dome-covered rooms enclosing large open courtyards. Since most of the teaching at the school would take place either in the prayer hall or, weather permitting, outside, all but one of the rooms in the medrese were for student accommodation. The exception was the dershane, a large lecture hall that would also house His Excellency's fine collection of books.

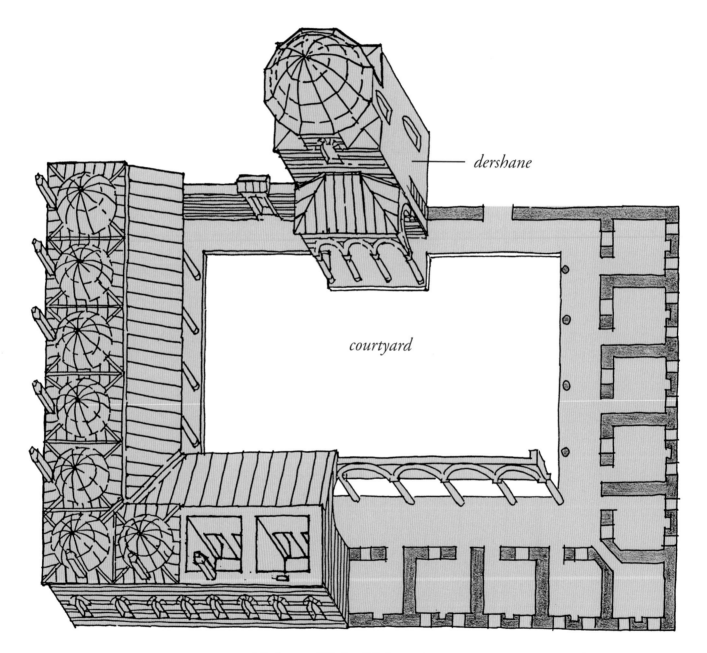

dershane

courtyard

Medrese of Suha Mehmet Pasa

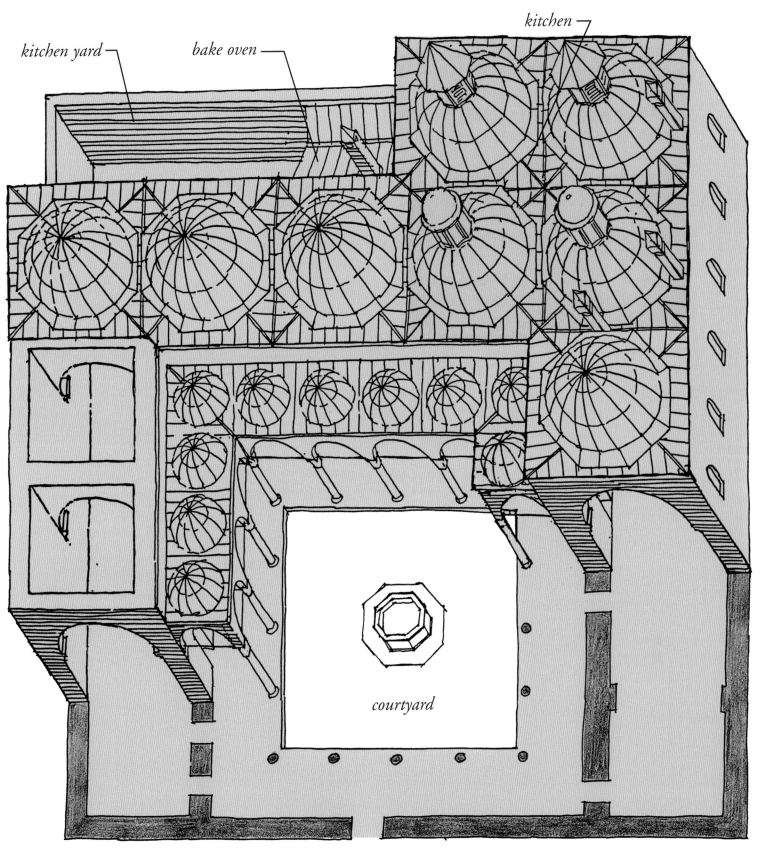

Imaret of Suha Mehmet Pasa

While the mosque would join the hearts and minds of the faithful through their devotion to God, the imaret would link the community within the kulliye to the community outside through their stomachs. All the rooms leading off the courtyard were dining rooms in which the staff and students of the complex would be fed, along with the poor and needy of the neighborhood. At the rear of the building, farthest away from the mosque, Agha had placed the large kitchen, complete with its own bakery.

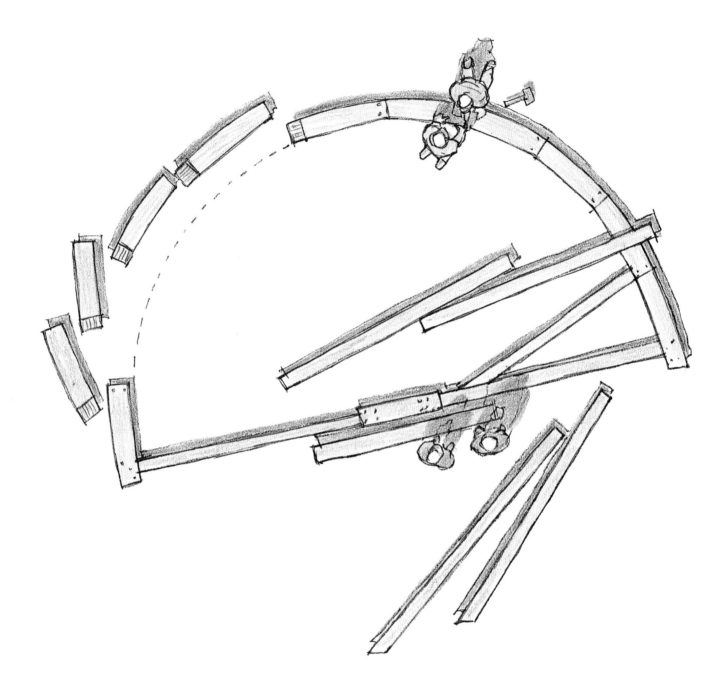

High above the prayer hall, Agha employed a third method for determining the shape and proportion of the great dome. Rather than using a single pole, which might prove less reliable at this scale, or having to build and support a heavy wooden form high up in the scaffolding, he instructed his carpenters to create a flat semicircular arch that would be rigid enough to maintain its shape and yet light enough to rotate easily on a fixed iron support. The form was first assembled on the ground and checked for accuracy. It was then taken apart and hoisted piece by piece to the top of the central scaffolding, where it was carefully reassembled and set onto its pivot.

While the thickness of the upper half of the dome would be established by the dimensions of the bricks used in its construction, the base would have to be made considerably wider. Not only did it have to resist the outward-pushing forces within the dome, but it also had to compensate for weight sacrificed to window openings. An interconnected ring of heavy iron bars was embedded near the tops of these windows to provide additional strength.

Bricklayers working at both ends of the wooden form carefully set each brick on a thick bed of mortar. To prevent the bricks from slipping, small wedges of brick were inserted between them. When a complete ring of bricks was in place and its mortar had sufficiently hardened any temporary supports could be removed. At this point, the finished course was capable of supporting itself and the next course could be safely built on top of it.

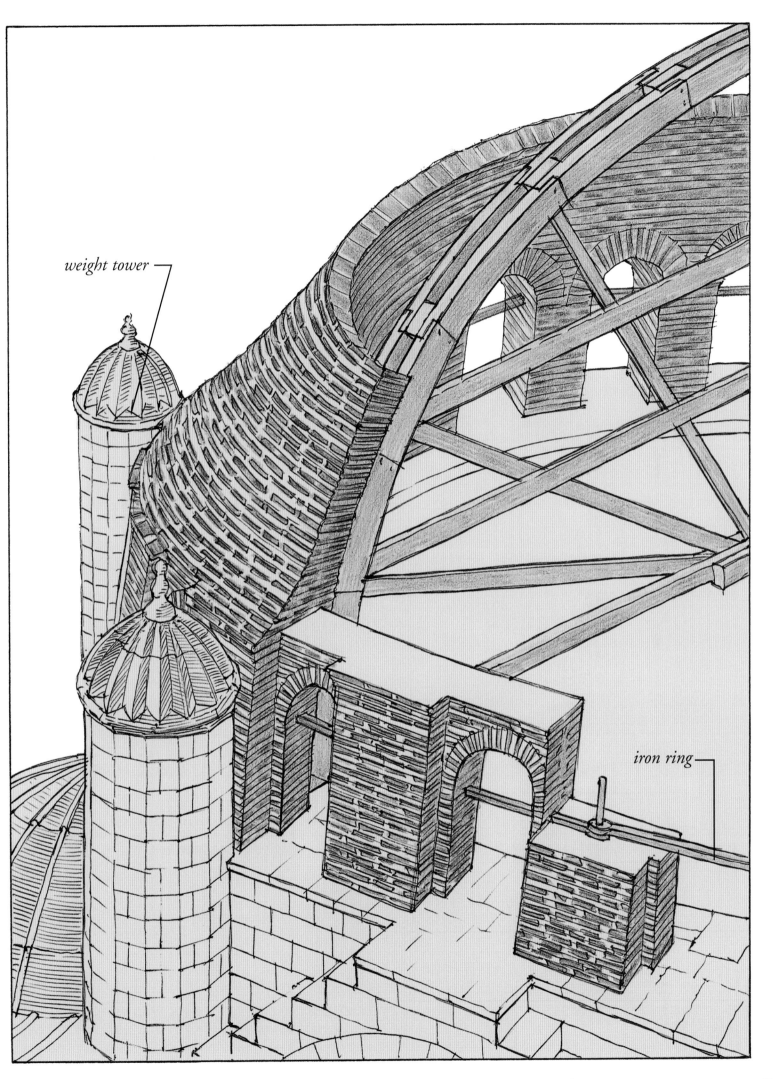

weight tower

iron ring

63

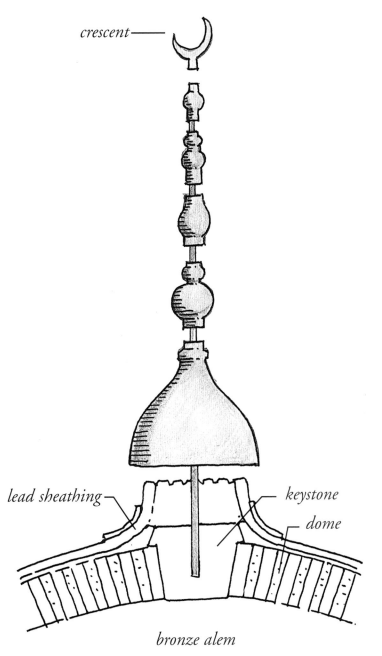

crescent——

lead sheathing——

——*keystone*

——*dome*

bronze alem

Over the following months, the circle of sky at the top of the dome continued to shrink. The last bit of light was finally snuffed out with the insertion of the keystone. By early spring, the entire hemisphere stood sheathed and waiting for the ceremony accompanying the installation of its bronze alem. There was great excitement as each piece was slipped carefully over the iron rod set into the keystone.

Cheers rose from every corner of the site when the gilded crescent was finally added. The admiral had a number of sons, who this time had accompanied him, distributing presents to the workers.

Although it would be several more months before the mosque was completely finished and even longer before the entire complex was operating, employees of the foundation's various programs, including those who would help maintain the buildings, had already been hired. Upon the recommendation of the ulema, a body of the most respected scholars of the Koran, the admiral had engaged a distinguished imam to lead the prayers and serve as one of the teachers in the medrese. Included among the scores of additional employees were more teachers, muezzins, clerks, caretakers, gardeners, lamplighters, and even a librarian. With its staff now assembled, the foundation's official deed was finally recorded on April 3, 1600.

Turbe of Suha Mehmet Pasa

After the ceremony, the admiral paid a brief visit to the site of his turbe, the foundations of which were already rising on the kibla behind the prayer hall. In accordance with his client's wishes, Agha had designed an octagonal building of great simplicity.

Now that the prayer hall was completely sealed against the elements, full attention could be given to the adornment of its interior surfaces. By tradition, all the decoration was to be drawn from three sources—the words of the Koran, natural vegetation, and the order and complexity of geometry.

Much of this decoration was painted and baked onto ceramic tiles. The rest would either be painted on or carved into plaster, stone, or wood. Akif Agha gave instructions about the general placement of decoration and the materials to be used, as well as the choices of text to be included. He left such decisions as specific patterns, shapes, and colors to the experienced craftsmen who would carry out the work.

Once the size and shape of a calligraphic panel had been determined, the selected text was written full size in Arabic. The finished sheets of paper were then passed along to an artisan who carefully traced the outline of each stroke with a row of pinholes. Coal dust pressed through the pinholes would leave a precise outline to guide each craftsman in his work.

1.

2.

3.

4.

Most of the ceramic tiles were imported from the famous kilns of Iznik in Anatolia. In addition to the blue and white calligraphic panels, their craftsmen also created richly colored tiles based on the lines and shapes of various flowers and vines.

In the painted decoration of the central dome, floral designs were combined with text. To underscore the significance of the words, a layer of glue was applied to each letter and then painstakingly covered with gold dust.

Elsewhere in the prayer hall, a variety of geometric patterns was being completed, from the capitals of the columns and piers, to the stone railings running along the galleries, to the ceilings beneath them.

Artisans in another part of the city were putting the final touches on pieces of the minber. Elaborate geometric patterns had been fashioned from hundreds of small pieces of wood while areas of carved decoration filled the remaining space.

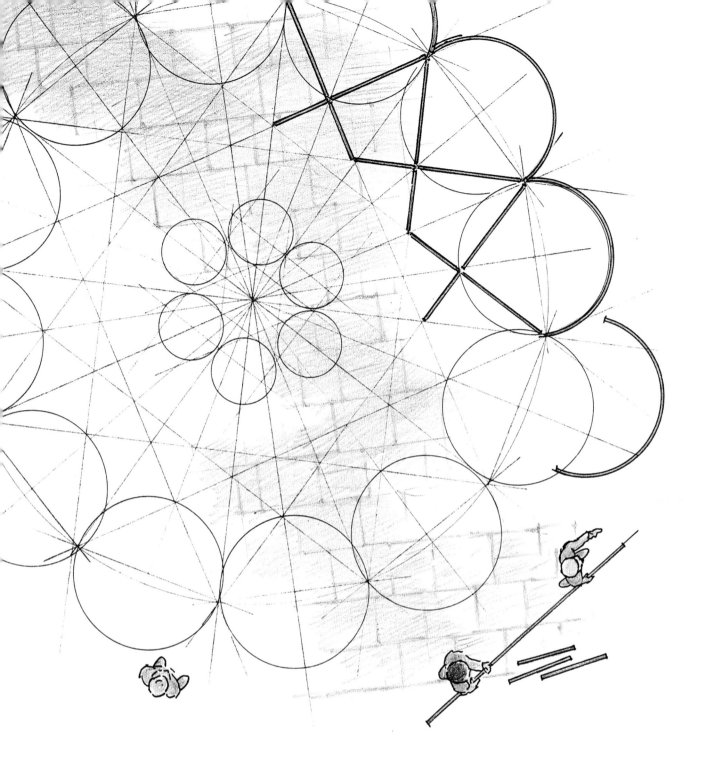

At another workshop, a pattern had been drawn on the floor to serve as a guide for the fabrication of the great chandelier that would eventually hang over the center of the prayer hall. This large iron frame would support a constellation of oil lamps above the heads of the worshipers.

Since the mihrab was the primary focus of attention during prayer, it and the wall around it naturally received the greatest concentration of decoration. The marble-lined mihrab was recessed between two false columns and below a gilded stone pediment. The stalactite carvings with which the mihrab culminated were also covered in gold. A collection of the finest floral and calligraphic tiles filled the entire space up to and surrounding the three stained-glass windows, which appeared to float below the semidome.

When the prayer hall was at last free of scaffolding, the ground was compacted, covered with a bed of cement, and finished with a layer of tiles.

On July 27, 1600, almost three years after the ceremonial placement of the mihrab, the completed mosque was dedicated. Joining the admiral and his family were representatives of the court, the military, and the ulema. Also in attendance were members of the various guilds that had worked on the buildings, including Huseyin Bey and all nine of his sons, several of Akif Agha's assistants from the office of the Court Architect, and assorted members of the local community.

Following ablutions, the entire entourage moved from the sadirvan to the portico, where they removed their shoes. As the admiral's wives and daughters turned toward the stairwell leading to the women's gallery, Suha Mehmet Pasa led the men through the main portal and into the prayer hall.

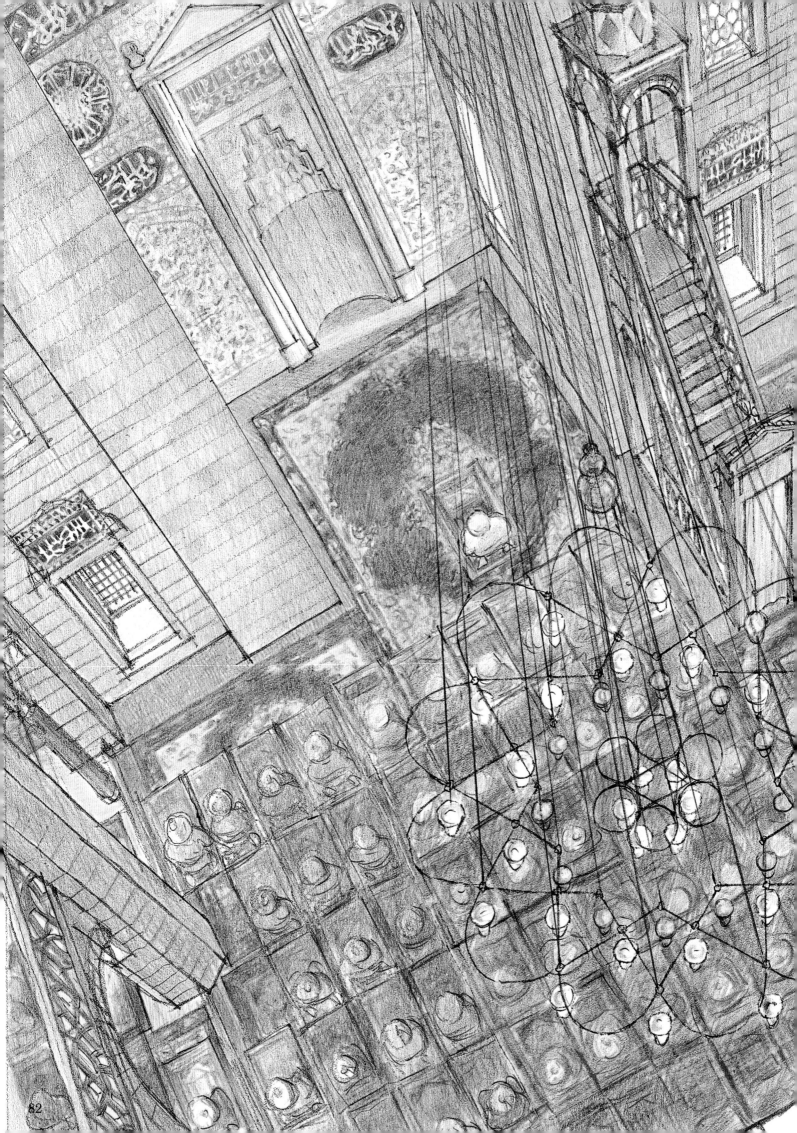

Bathed in light filtering through countless pieces of colored glass, they slowly moved across the sea of carpets that covered the floor. As the assembled placed their prayer mats side by side and end to end, their eyes were drawn upward past the sparkling tiles and radiant gilding, past the deeply cut panels of stalactite carving, to Agha's great dome which seemed to float weightlessly above them. Most were still admiring their surroundings as Suha Mehmet Pasa climbed the steps of the minber to give his speech. After thanking all those who had, with God's help, transformed his vision into reality, the proud yet humbled admiral returned to his place facing the kibla wall. Then as the imam lead the congregation in prayer, the splendor of the architecture in which they were gathered temporarily faded. Each worshiper now entered a more intimate space—a space defined entirely and fully by the five positions of prayer within the borders of his own prayer mat.

While the decorators had been at work inside the prayer hall, the adjacent medrese had been completed. Each of its simply finished rooms, which now housed up to three students, had its own fireplace, pair of windows, and recessed shelves for a few personal belongings.

The imaret, on the other hand, had proven to be more of a challenge. Due to the slope of the site and the instability of the soil, it had been necessary first to construct a large vaulted basement under almost half of the building. It wasn't until October 15, 1600, that Agha and Bey finally toured the finished structure. In the all-important kitchen, they found the staff of the imaret busily preparing the midday meal. Smoke from beneath great caldrons of simmering soup rose toward the carefully placed vents that rested on two of the four domes spanning the kitchen. The other two had been capped by window-filled cupolas to admit more light into the space. As workers scurried back and forth with food for the tables and fuel for the fires, the smell of freshly baked bread mixed with that of soup and spices to fill the air. Above the chatter and clattering of pots and pans, the rumbling of a large grinding wheel could just be heard from the kitchen yard.

On his way back to the office, a well-fed Akif Agha walked past the cesme, which he had set into the prescinct wall facing the imaret. From the moment the first cool water had flowed into the stone basin, it had become one of the most popular gathering places in the neighborhood — a sight that gave the architect particular pleasure.

Two weeks later, as Agha was overseeing the installation of the doors to the recently completed turbe, word reached him that the admiral had been stricken —apparently as he reached for figs in his cherished garden—and had departed this earth for the rewards of an even greater paradise. The admiral's remains were soon resting in the ground beneath his empty cloth-draped coffin.

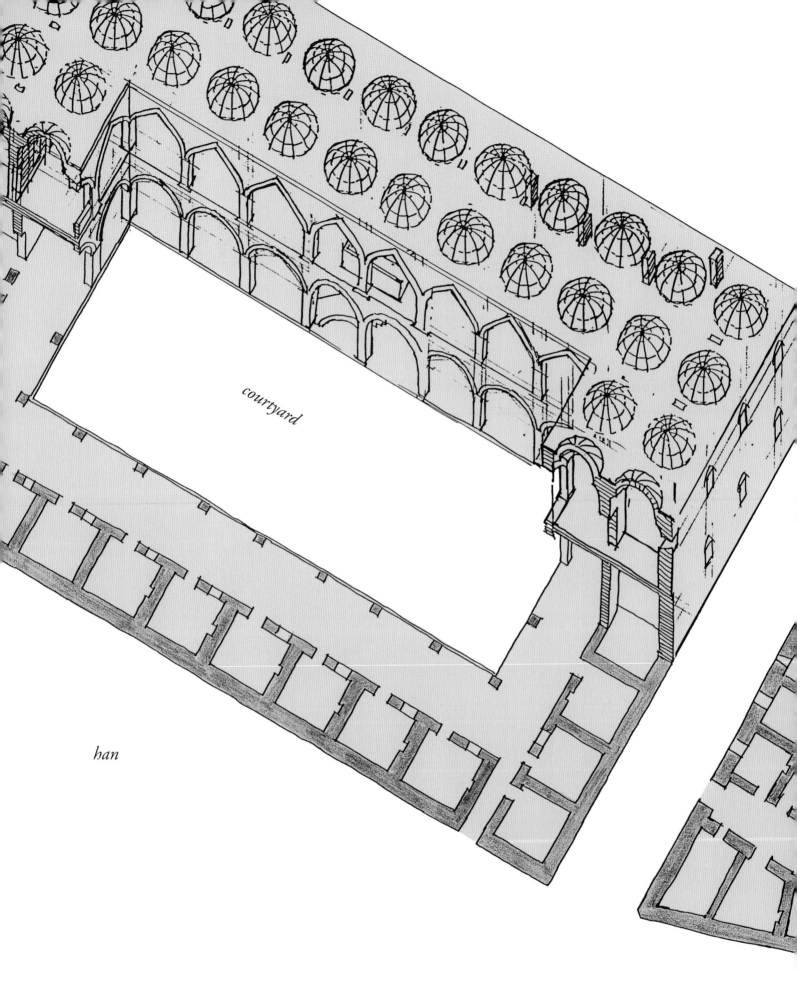

courtyard

han

Han and Caravanserai of Suha Mehmet Pasa

With his patron's passing, Akif Agha had naturally assumed that his work on the old man's behalf was complete. Several months after Suha Mehmet Pasa's death, however, he was informed that the admiral's favorite wife, who was also one of the sultan's many cousins, wished to ensure her late husband's legacy by adding a han and a caravanserai to the kulliye. Over the years these two buildings would generate income to help support the activities of the foundation.

The ground floor of the han would be rented out to local businessmen and artisans. The second level would offer accommodations to out-of-town guests and bachelors. The second level of the caravanserai would also offer accommodations, but this time to caravan drivers. Their beasts were to be housed in a large vaulted stable below. Whereas the han was placed next to the imaret, Agha located the caravanserai farther from the prayer hall and along a busy street close to the harbor. The rooms of both buildings were once again laid out around courtyards. Not only would this arrangement provide a secure outdoor gathering place, but it would ensure that plenty of light and air reached all of the surrounding rooms.

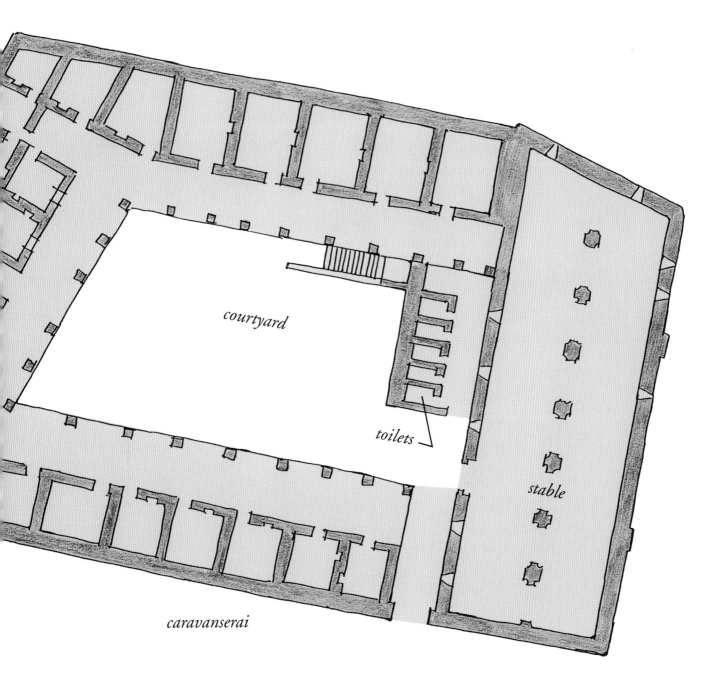

courtyard

toilets

stable

caravanserai

Leaving the project in Bey's reliable hands, Akif Agha spent most of the next two years away from the city. Part of that time was spent participating in the hajj, the great pilgrimage to Mecca that all able-bodied Muslims were expected to make. The remainder was spent either overseeing repairs to the extensive supply system that brought water to Istanbul or working on commissions for several of the sultan's most important ministers and viziers.

By the time Agha settled back into city life, the han and the caravanserai were not only finished but flourishing. The surrounding streets were once again clogged with carts. Though now, instead of stone and scaffolding, they were laden with baskets of fruit, bundles of flowers and precious woods, bolts of richly colored fabric, and sacks of fragrant spices. Even the narrow side streets were filled with activity. Tinsmiths and cloth merchants sold their wares from beneath the awnings over the entrances to their shops. Hawkers and performers vied for customers. Glasses of tea were filled and sold from urns carried on the backs of a handful of wandering vendors. Children ran among soldiers and holy men, travelers mixed with locals. Several times a day, the cacophony of the streets was tempered by the periodic call to prayer from the muezzin's balcony.

When completed, the kulliye of Suha Mehmet Pasa officially comprised seven buildings, but unofficially it had spawned hundreds more. New houses, shops, workshops, factories, warehouses, and countless large and small gardens now filled the surrounding plots of land where charred timber and burned bricks had once been piled. Though memories of the great fire undoubtedly lingered, all the ashes had long ago become part of the soil upon which new life was now thriving.

GLOSSARY

ALEM

The finial placed on top of a dome or minaret.

CAPITAL

The crowning piece that sits directly on top of a column.

CARAVANSERAI

An overnight stopping place for caravans that provided safe accommodation for both the drivers and the animals.

CENTERING

The temporary wooden support over which the stones of an arch were laid.

CESME

A public drinking fountain.

CISTERN

A tank for storing water.

CUPOLA

A small domed structure crowning a larger dome or roof and often filled with windows.

DOME

An arched ceiling of even curvature built on a circular base.

FALSE DOME

A structure with the form of a dome on the outside but supported on the inside with wood or masonry.

FORGE

Both the furnace in which metal is heated to a high temperature and the workshop in which heated metal is shaped into various objects by hammering.

HAMAM

A public bathhouse containing cold, warm, and hot rooms.

HAN

A two-story building in which space could be rented for conducting business and for accommodation.

IMAM

The man who leads the congregation in prayer.

IMARET

Soup kitchen and public dining rooms.

ISLAM

The religion of Muslims based on the teachings of Muhammad.

KAABA

The great shrine in Mecca that all Muslims face when praying.

KEYSTONE

The central stone of an arch.

KIBLA

The direction of Mecca.

KIBLA WALL

The front wall of a prayer hall always located perpendicular to the kibla.

KORAN

The sacred text of Islam.

KULLIYE

The complex of buildings associated with a charitable foundation and its mosque.

MECCA

The birthplace of the prophet Muhammad.

MEDRESE

A college for Muslim education.

MIHRAB

The niche in the center of the kibla wall indicating the direction of Mecca, from in front of which the imam leads the prayers.

MINARET

The tower from which Muslims are called to prayer five times a day.

MINBER

The high, stepped pulpit used for sermons at Friday services.

MUEZZIN

A cantor who calls the faithful to prayer from the minaret.

MUSLIM

A person who believes in and practices the faith of Islam.

PENDENTIVE

A concave support built out from a corner to help form a circular base for the dome above.

PIER

A vertical support built up of stone or brick.

PORTICO

A high covered entry area.

SADIRVAN

A fountain associated with a mosque and usually located in the center of the courtyard. It contains a cistern in which water is stored for ablutions—the ritual washing of the hands and feet or entire body.

SEMIDOME

Half a dome.

STALACTITE

A style of ornate decoration in which rows of ornamentation are, or appear to be, supported upon another from the narrowest at the bottom to the widest at the top.

SULTAN

The supreme ruler of a Muslim country, head of the Ottoman Empire.

TURBE

Tomb.

ULEMA

The council of the most learned Koran scholars.